This Keepsake Journal was given to

———————————————————

by

———————————————————

Date

———————————————————

A Keepsake Journal of Books Read to Me

Created and Written by Emily Ellison

Longstreet Press
Atlanta, Georgia

Published by
LONGSTREET PRESS, INC.
A Subsidiary of Cox Newspapers,
A division of Cox Enterprises, Inc.
2140 Newmarket Parkway
Suite 118
Marietta, GA 30067

Printed in the United States of America
Electronic film prep and separations by Advertising Technologies, Inc., Atlanta, GA

1st printing 1995

Library of Congress Catalog Card Number: 95-77245

ISBN 1-56352-258-6

Illustrations by Vickey Bolling
Jacket and book design by Vickey Bolling and Elaine Streithof

*or*

my father,

who read to me when I was a child,

and for

my daughter,

who reads to me now.

"When you read to a child, when you put a book in a child's hands,

you are bringing that child news of the infinitely varied nature of life.

You are an awakener."

—Paula Fox
1974 Newberry Award winner
for THE SLAVE DANCER

The Small, Quiet Hours
of the Life of a Child

*H*ere sits my father at the edge of my bed, reading. His southern voice is soft and slow, at times halting, but always soothing. Sometimes I follow his finger as it moves beneath the words along the page, but mostly I watch a little bubble of skin (like a tiny pellet under the flesh) ride up and down on his lower lip as he speaks. I follow it up and down, up and down, through the hills and valleys of language. Every movement my father makes, every stop and start and turn of his voice is fascinating to me. He puts an index finger to his tongue, moistens the top corner of the right-hand page, and pulls the story along.

There is nothing in the world as peaceful and comforting and safe as this, and when he looks up and makes the move to close the book for the night, I beg for one more chapter. One more page, then! Just a few more *words*.

Whenever I am asked, as writers always are, whether or not I was read to as a child, this image comes back to me as vividly as crisp black type on clean white bond. I was indeed read to nightly when I was a child. But it was only after I had a child of my own, only when I began reading to her from the countless nursery rhymes and fairy tales and picture books given to us by friends and later found at libraries and book stores, that I realized my father had not served me *typical* fare.

I don't know if it was because he wasn't sure what was appropriate reading material for a six- (seven, eight, nine, and ten-) year-old like me, with such an appetite for words and his companionship, or if it was because in his over-worked day-to-day life he had not a minute to spare hunting up children's literature. My guess is that it was a little of both. My guess, too, is that since he was zealously pragmatic and a reader himself, he decided to make the most of valuable "down" time and kill the proverbial two birds with one book. Whatever his reasoning, my father read to me whatever *he* was reading.

There were the paperback biographies of great men, such as Marco Polo, Lou Gehrig, Abraham Lincoln, and King David. Often it was the evening newspaper I got, or the Bible, or one of his own poems. Sometimes it was entire blocks of text from the cordovan-colored set of *American People's Encyclopedia* that lined a long shelf in our living room, something about the giant stone statues on Easter Island, perhaps, or the pyramids in Egypt, or the Great Wall of China.

I realize now, of course, that Daddy could have been reading catalog copy to me, or the backs of cereal boxes, or the directions for laying drainage pipe. It wouldn't have mattered. What did matter was that he took time away from his endless work, from his countless chores, to sit so still with *me*. There were no distractions when he read, nothing pulled his focus from the brave souls, the craggy faces, the candlelit cabins, the rocky battlefields, the dusty ball parks that so enthralled him. And, thus enthralled, he was not pulled from the daughter who adored him. Though I doubt he knew it, that tender time alone with my father, quietly listening to words, became the most precious hours of my life as a child.

Although it was the *time* with my father that I treasured, the words he read were not superfluous. They introduced me to personalities and places I would never have known without them. They gave me vocabulary I could never have heard in conversations with the people around me in the Carolinas, Georgia, and south Florida. They immersed me in cultures and eras that otherwise would have remained forever hidden between the covers of books. They gave me an instinctive knowledge of syntax and a love for the rhythm of the English language. And, without *my* being aware of it, they provided a structure on which all the rest of my learning would be built. Those words formed a bridge to the words I myself would later read, and eventually write.

*H*ere I sit in an over-sized, wooden rocking chair, cradling my infant daughter in one arm while holding in my other hand the bold reds, greens, yellows, and blues of *Goodnight Moon*. Here is my daughter as a toddler, sitting beside me on a thread-worn love seat and following the antics and adventures of Frog and Toad. Here we lie together on her creaking iron bed as I read to her about stalwart little Abel alone on an island.

It begins to dawn on me that most children's bedtime reading material does not come from encyclopedias. It begins to dawn on me that there is a big plug missing in what author Jim Trelease calls my "cultural core of stories."

Once I am aware of the plug, I begin filling it enthusiastically. At the start, I seem to be under the impression I am reading all these children's books for the benefit of my young daughter. But soon I learn I am really doing it for me. When I run across a new author, such as William Steig or Natalie Babbitt or Randall Jarrell or Eleanor Estes, I read them with the same kind of hungry pleasure that years ago I read an adult author that was new to me such as John Cheever or Anne Tyler or Ralph Ellison or Mary Gordon.

Something else I learn. Not all children sit so passively as I did while they are read to. My daughter is an incredible critic! She doesn't put up with dull dialogue or unsatisfying endings. If a book doesn't hold her attention the first time, she doesn't want it read again. She's not much for sentimentality, or sloppy plots. She likes clever conversation, snappy vocabulary, gorgeous pictures, believable characters, and lots of irreverence and humor.

Once, when she was maybe two or three, she placed on the floor a large picture book — one with particularly beautiful paintings — stood on the open book, and said, "I want in there." I thought I would never forget the name of that book. But I have.

Another time, when she was probably four or five, we finished a story and realized there was no real resolution for the character. She threw the book across the room and said, "That is so *stupid!*" She was right. Unfortunately, I can't remember the name of that book either.

Now, after all these years of reading, after all these thousands of books, I wish I had written down their titles and made note of the things my daughter liked or disliked about them. I wish I had a list of the stories she begged for again and again, the ones that we laughed over, and the ones that made us hold each other and cry. I wish, too, that I had a record of the books my father read to me and maybe a few comments, written in his tight, blocky hand, of some of the things he and I might have thought and said.

I can't remember my mother reading to me at all. But that may be simply because, like most children of the fifties and sixties, the majority of my hours were spent with her, and thus our time together was taken for granted and did not seem so remarkable as the few minutes I had each day with my father. Once again, if Mother *did* read to me, I wish there was something recorded somewhere that said what the stories were and when and where she read them.

For these reasons (along with my emphatic belief that reading aloud to children is a singular blessing), I created this journal for parents, grandparents, godparents, baby-sitters, friends, older siblings, teachers, and others to record the books they read to the children in their lives. The time it takes to read to a child is so small. But when added together, over the length of a childhood, the benefits of that time — for both child and adult — are enormous.

The gifts my father gave me when I was a child are many. Yet of all the things he provided — the piano and ballet and drama lessons, the trips, the clothes, the bicycles and toys, the summer camps, the education — none of those things remains as significant to me today, nor as cherished, as those small, quiet hours when I followed his voice through the bumps and turns and twists of language and was time and again lifted from my bed, swept out of our house, and was shown the world.

Name of book _____

Author _____

Date read _____ Read by _____

Comments _____

_____

Name of book _____

Author _____

Date read _____ Read by _____

Comments _____

_____

Name of book _____

Author _____

Date read _____ Read by _____

Comments _____

_____

Name of book _____

Author _____

Date read _____ Read by _____

Comments _____

_____

Name of book _____

Author _____

Date read _____ Read by _____

Comments _____

_____

There was a woman in my town, Mrs. Flowers, who would read to me in a
mellifluous voice. She loved poetry and through her reading I eventually began to
speak again. She read Dickens to me and I lived in London.
She read me the Brontë sisters and I walked with them on the moors.
By the time I was 11, I had lived all those different lives.

— Maya Angelou

Name of book ....

Author ....

Date read .... Read by ....

Comments ....

....

Name of book ....

Author ....

Date read .... Read by ....

Comments ....

....

Name of book _____

Author _____

Date read _____ Read by _____

Comments _____

_____

Name of book _____

Author _____

Date read _____ Read by _____

Comments _____

_____

Name of book _____

Author _____

Date read _____ Read by _____

Comments _____

_____

_____

Name of book _____

Author _____

Date read _____ Read by _____

Comments _____

_____

_____

Name of book _____

Author _____

Date read _____ Read by _____

Comments _____

_____

According to child psychologist Dr. Bruno Bettelheim, a mother once approached Albert Einstein and asked, "What should my child study to grow up to be smart and famous like you?"

Dr. Einstein answered, "Fairy tales."

"Fairy tales? But I mean, what important books should he read?"

"Fairy tales."

"But how will he then become a great scientist?" the woman persisted.

"Surely, you can suggest some meaningful works."

"Madam, the answer is fairy tales, fairy tales, and more fairy tales."

Name of book _____

Author _____

Date read _____ Read by _____

Comments _____

_____

Name of book _____

Author _____

Date read _____ Read by _____

Comments _____

_____

Name of book _____

Author _____

Date read _____ Read by _____

Comments _____

_____

Name of book _____

Author _____

Date read _____ Read by _____

Comments _____

_____

Name of book _____

Author _____

Date read _____ Read by _____

Comments _____

_____

_____

Name of book _____

Author _____

Date read _____ Read by _____

Comments _____

_____

_____

Name of book _____

Author _____

Date read _____ Read by _____

Comments _____

_____

_____

In October of 1945, for my 4th birthday, I was given a plaster doll, a tin suitcase and a copy of "The Little House" by Virginia Lee Burton. The doll was later passed on to someone else and the suitcase was lost in a move, but I still have "The Little House." I don't mean I just keep it stashed away somewhere; I mean I still use it. It stays where I can pull it out any time I want to. And I often want to.

— Anne Tyler

Name of book ....

Author ....

Date read .... Read by ....

Comments ....

....

Name of book ....

Author ....

Date read .... Read by ....

Comments ....

....

Name of book _____

Author _____

Date read _____ Read by _____

Comments _____

_____

Name of book _____

Author _____

Date read _____ Read by _____

Comments _____

_____

Name of book ....

Author ....

Date read .... Read by ....

Comments ....

....

Name of book ....

Author ....

Date read .... Read by ....

Comments ....

....

Name of book _____

Author _____

Date read _____ Read by _____

Comments _____

_____

Books swept me away, one after the other, this way and that;
I made endless vows according to their lights, for I believed them.

— Annie Dillard
AN AMERICAN CHILDHOOD

Name of book _____

Author _____

Date read _____ Read by _____

Comments _____

_____

Name of book _____

Author _____

Date read _____ Read by _____

Comments _____

_____

Name of book _____

Author _____

Date read _____ Read by _____

Comments _____

_____

Name of book _____

Author _____

Date read _____ Read by _____

Comments _____

_____

Name of book _____

Author _____

Date read _____ Read by _____

Comments _____

_____

Name of book _____

Author _____

Date read _____ Read by _____

Comments _____

_____

Name of book _____

Author _____

Date read _____ Read by _____

Comments _____

_____

_____

*It is a great thing to start life with a small number of
really good books which are your very own.*

— Sherlock Holmes

Name of book _____

Author _____

Date read _____ **R**ead by _____

Comments _____

_____

Name of book _____

Author _____

Date read _____ **R**ead by _____

Comments _____

_____

Name of book _____

Author _____

Date read _____ Read by _____

Comments _____

_____

Name of book _____

Author _____

Date read _____ Read by _____

Comments _____

_____

Name of book _____

Author _____

Date read _____ Read by _____

Comments _____

_____

Name of book _____

Author _____

Date read _____ Read by _____

Comments _____

_____

Name of book _____

Author _____

Date read _____ Read by _____

Comments _____

_____

*If we prescribe books as medicine, our children have a perfect right
to refuse the nasty-tasting spoon.*

— Newbery Medal-winner Katherine Paterson
Author of THE GREAT GILLY HOPKINS

Name of book _____

Author _____

Date read _____ Read by _____

Comments _____

_____

Name of book _____

Author _____

Date read _____ Read by _____

Comments _____

_____

Name of book _____

Author _____

Date read _____ **Read by** _____

Comments _____

_____

Name of book _____

Author _____

Date read _____ **Read by** _____

Comments _____

_____

Name of book _____

Author _____

Date read _____   Read by _____

Comments _____

_____

Name of book _____

Author _____

Date read _____   Read by _____

Comments _____

_____

Name of book _____

Author _____

Date read _____ Read by _____

Comments _____

_____

When I am brought low by the vicissitudes of life,

I stumble to my bookshelves. I take a little dose of Zemach or Schulevitz.

I grab a shot of Goffstein or Marshall. I medicate myself with Steig or Sendak, and the treatment works.

I always feel much better.

— Arnold Lobel

Name of book _____

Author _____

Date read _____ Read by _____

Comments _____

_____

Name of book _____

Author _____

Date read _____ Read by _____

Comments _____

_____

Name of book _____

Author _____

Date read _____ Read by _____

Comments _____

_____

Name of book _____

Author _____

Date read _____ Read by _____

Comments _____

_____

Name of book _____

Author _____

Date read _____ Read by _____

Comments _____

_____

Name of book _____

Author _____

Date read _____ Read by _____

Comments _____

_____

Name of book

Author

Date read   Read by

Comments

It took me years to understand that words are often as important as experience,
because words make experiences last.

— Willie Morris,
NORTH TOWARD HOME

Name of book _____

Author _____

Date read _____ Read by _____

Comments _____

_____

Name of book _____

Author _____

Date read _____ Read by _____

Comments _____

_____

Name of book ....

Author ....

Date read .... Read by ....

Comments ....

....

Name of book ....

Author ....

Date read .... Read by ....

Comments ....

....

Name of book _____

Author _____

Date read _____ Read by _____

Comments _____

_____

Name of book _____

Author _____

Date read _____ Read by _____

Comments _____

_____

Name of book _____

Author _____

Date read _____ Read by _____

Comments _____

_____

When I was 10, I was in the hospital briefly, with pneumonia. It was grand.
The pain was over before I got there, where I had my mother (Anne Morrow Lindbergh) all to myself.

She's a great reader-aloud; to have her all to myself was wonderful.

— Anne Lindbergh

Name of book _____

Author _____

Date read _____ Read by _____

Comments _____

_____

Name of book _____

Author _____

Date read _____ Read by _____

Comments _____

_____

Name of book _____

Author _____

Date read _____ Read by _____

Comments _____

_____

Name of book _____

Author _____

Date read _____ Read by _____

Comments _____

_____

Name of book _____

Author _____

Date read _____ Read by _____

Comments _____

_____

Name of book _____

Author _____

Date read _____ Read by _____

Comments _____

_____

Name of book _____

Author _____

Date read _____ Read by _____

Comments _____

_____

The library is not a shrine for the worship of books. It is not a temple where literary
incense must be burned or where one's devotion to the bound books is expressed in ritual.
A library, to modify the famous metaphor of Socrates, should be the delivery room for the birth of ideas. . . .

— Norman Cousins

Name of book _____

Author _____

Date read _____ Read by _____

Comments _____

_____

Name of book _____

Author _____

Date read _____ Read by _____

Comments _____

_____

Name of book _____

Author _____

Date read _____ Read by _____

Comments _____

_____

Name of book _____

Author _____

Date read _____ Read by _____

Comments _____

_____

Name of book

Author

Date read _____ **Read by** _____

Comments

Name of book

Author

Date read _____ **Read by** _____

Comments

Name of book _____

Author _____

Date read _____ Read by _____

Comments _____

_____

I believe a child reads as he runs and swims,
because he can, with compulsive joy in the act.

— Ellen Douglas

Name of book _____

Author _____

Date read _____ **R**ead by _____

Comments _____

_____

Name of book _____

Author _____

Date read _____ **R**ead by _____

Comments _____

_____

Name of book _____

Author _____

Date read _____ Read by _____

Comments _____

_____

Name of book _____

Author _____

Date read _____ Read by _____

Comments _____

_____

Name of book _____

Author _____

Date read _____ Read by _____

Comments _____

_____

Name of book _____

Author _____

Date read _____ Read by _____

Comments _____

_____

Name of book _____

Author _____

Date read _____ Read by _____

Comments _____

_____

I came to appreciate what good books really were and realized how much
I needed them and they gradually gave me a stoical confidence in myself:
I was not alone in this world and I would not perish!

— Maxim Gorky
MY APPRENTICESHIP

Name of book _____

Author _____

Date read _____ Read by _____

Comments _____

_____

_____

Name of book _____

Author _____

Date read _____ Read by _____

Comments _____

_____

_____

Name of book _____

Author _____

Date read _____ Read by _____

Comments _____

_____

Name of book _____

Author _____

Date read _____ Read by _____

Comments _____

_____

Name of book _____

Author _____

Date read _____ Read by _____

Comments _____

_____

Name of book _____

Author _____

Date read _____ Read by _____

Comments _____

_____

Name of book _____

Author _____

Date read _____ Read by _____

Comments _____

_____

_____

When I was a child, a relative gave me IVANHOE to grow into.

I was so disappointed that I still have not grown into it.

— Beverly Cleary
author of ROMONA THE PEST

Name of book _____

Author _____

Date read _____ Read by _____

Comments _____

_____

Name of book _____

Author _____

Date read _____ Read by _____

Comments _____

_____

Name of book _____

Author _____

Date read _____ **R**ead by _____

Comments _____

_____

Name of book _____

Author _____

Date read _____ **R**ead by _____

Comments _____

_____

Name of book _____

Author _____

Date read _____ Read by _____

Comments _____

_____

Name of book _____

Author _____

Date read _____ Read by _____

Comments _____

_____

Name of book ....

Author ....

Date read .... Read by ....

Comments ....

....

I learned from the age of two or three that any room in our house, at any time of day,

was there to read in, or to be read to. My mother read to me. She'd read to me in the

big bedroom in the mornings, when we were in her rocker together, which ticked in rhythm as we rocked,

as though we had a cricket accompanying the story. . . . She was an expressive reader. When she was reading

PUSS IN BOOTS, for instance, it was impossible not to know that she distrusted all cats.

— Eudora Welty

Name of book _____

Author _____

Date read _____ Read by _____

Comments _____

_____

Name of book _____

Author _____

Date read _____ Read by _____

Comments _____

_____

Name of book _____

Author _____

Date read _____ Read by _____

Comments _____

_____

Name of book _____

Author _____

Date read _____ Read by _____

Comments _____

_____

Name of book _____

Author _____

Date read _____ Read by _____

Comments _____

_____

Name of book _____

Author _____

Date read _____ Read by _____

Comments _____

_____

Name of book _____

Author _____

Date read _____ Read by _____

Comments _____

_____

My idea of a perfect afternoon was lying in front of the radio rereading my favorite Big Little Book, DICK TRACY MEETS STOOGE VILLER.

— Russell Baker,
GROWING UP

Name of book _____

Author _____

Date read _____ Read by _____

Comments _____

_____

Name of book _____

Author _____

Date read _____ Read by _____

Comments _____

_____

Name of book _____

Author _____

Date read _____ Read by _____

Comments _____

_____

Name of book _____

Author _____

Date read _____ Read by _____

Comments _____

_____

Name of book _____

Author _____

Date read _____ Read by _____

Comments _____

_____

Name of book _____

Author _____

Date read _____ Read by _____

Comments _____

_____

Name of book _____

Author _____

Date read _____ Read by _____

Comments _____

_____

Books were far more than an amusement in my childhood; they were my other lives,

and this visible existence I now lead in the workaday world was touched and transformed by them forever.

The spell was never broken; all through my adult life, children's literature has given me unabated pleasure. . .

and confirmed my belief that a child's life without books read for pleasure is a child's life deprived.

— Michele Landsberg
READING FOR THE LOVE OF IT: BEST BOOKS FOR CHILDREN

Name of book _____

Author _____

Date read _____ Read by _____

Comments _____

_____

Name of book _____

Author _____

Date read _____ Read by _____

Comments _____

_____

Name of book _____

Author _____

Date read _____ Read by _____

Comments _____

_____

Name of book _____

Author _____

Date read _____ Read by _____

Comments _____

_____

Reading Great Books to Children

*E*ducators and reading experts talk enthusiastically about the numerous benefits that come from reading aloud to children. But when they list these benefits, they usually do so as if all the profits fall to the listeners. In reality, so many of the rewards of reading to our daughter have gone to her father and me. After all, we're the ones who receive the credit for her impressive vocabulary (as if we are the ones who taught her words such as "runcible" and "schnozzola" and "confloption," instead of Edward Lear, William Steig, and Harve and Margot Zemach).

We get patted on the back for taking her to Spain and France and Russia and China, when it was actually Munro Leaf and Ludwig Bemelmans and Patricia Polacco and Marjorie Flack who took her. People think we are the ones who magically gave her access to such creatures as a bat-poet, a spelling spider, and a flying pig instead of the real magicians who did it: Randall Jarrell, E. B. White, and Susan Jeschke. We sit back and smugly take the credit for her loving a good joke when her sense of humor and respect for nonsense were really nurtured by William Joyce, Jon Sciezka, Jack Prelutsky, Dr. Seuss, and so many others. We sit back and rake in the praise for raising this curious and spirited and articulate child, when in reality we have had several hundred smart and talented people helping us every day. Sometimes I think what a lonely road parenthood would be without the assistance of all these wonderful authors and illustrators.

Here's another confession. Until I actually *read* children's literature, I didn't give it much weight. I thought books written for kids were somehow "less than" books written for older people: less work, less important, less likely to be art. I could not have been more wrong. Read a novel by Randall Jarrell, a poem by John Ciardi, a fantasy by Ursula K. LeGuin, or one page by M. B. Goffstein, and you know that the best writers for children indeed create art. Watch the effects of literature on children's verbal skills and comprehension, and you see that it is important. Try writing a really first-rate children's book yourself, and you darn sure learn that it is work.

Of course the real lessons and the true blessings of reading with our daughter have been in the sweet hours we've spent snuggled together having the times of our lives; in using the talents of others to rescue our own sometimes dormant imaginations; and in using stories to help us interpret human actions and feelings and understand the complexities of our world.

As I said in the beginning of this journal, I believe that children gain from having almost anything read to them. However, there is a tremendous range in the quality of books written for children, and I'm a firm believer in providing youngsters (and ourselves) with as much of the "good stuff" as possible. Children who are raised with great children's literature around them are the ones most likely to appreciate and expect the same quality in books they read as adults and the ones most likely to remain readers for their lifetimes.

Therefore, I'm including lists of some of our favorites. These books were chosen because they do an exceptional job of capturing both listeners' and readers' imagination and keeping them entertained. They were also chosen because of their wonderful characters (sometimes mice, sometimes men), the variety of subject matter, the perfect match of illustrations and text, and the superb quality of writing.

Since it is difficult to know the exact listening level for any one child, the books from one list may overlap the books from another: many preschoolers will be able to easily comprehend a book usually thought of as for older children, and some older students will still enjoy having books from the younger children's lists read and reread to them. There is also a fairly wide range of listening difficulty and length of text in each list, but the books were selected as carefully as possible for the emotional maturity and the general interests of children in that specific age group.

The suggested lists go only as far as the fifth grade not because that's when parents should stop reading to their children but because that's as far as I've gotten. At your local library and book stores you can find numerous other suggested reading lists for all ages of children, including the names of all Caldecott and Newberry Award winners, the annual Coretta Scott King Awards winners (given to African-American writers and illustrators), and Reading Rainbow books. The Children's Book Council also offers a free brochure listing "75 Authors and Illustrators Everyone Should Know."

If you are unfamiliar with children's literature, I hope these lists will get you started. The resource books on the last page will also provide you with the titles and authors of excellent books to satisfy the needs, interests, and personalities of every child. And if you haven't been to a library in a while, the codes listed below will help you locate nearly any children's book you're looking for.

Picture Books	(J Pic)
Easy Reading Books	(J Easy)
Fiction	(J)
Folk and Fairy Tales	(398 and 398.2)
Biographies	(JB)

Great Books for Reading to Infants and Toddlers

A, MY NAME IS ALICE by Jane E. Bayer

ALL FALL DOWN by Helen Oxenbury

ARE YOU MY MOTHER? by P. D. Eastman

BROWN BEAR BROWN BEAR, WHAT DO YOU SEE?
by Bill Martin, Jr.

EACH PEACH PEAR PLUM, AN "I SPY" STORY
by Janet and Allan Ahlberg

FISH EYES: A BOOK YOU CAN COUNT ON
by Lois Ehlert

FREIGHT TRAIN by Donald Crews

THE GINGERBREAD BOY by Paul Galdone

GOODNIGHT MOON by Margaret Wise Brown

HARRY THE DIRTY DOG by Gene Zion

HECTOR PROTECTOR AND AS I WENT OVER THE
WATER: TWO NURSERY RHYMES
by Maurice Sendak

A HOUSE IS A HOUSE FOR ME
by Mary Ann Hoberman

I CAN—CAN YOU? By Peggy Parish

IF YOU GIVE A MOUSE A COOKIE
by Laura Joffe Numeroff

THE LITTLE FUR FAMILY by Margaret Wise Brown

LITTLE RED RIDING HOOD by Trina Schart Hyman

LULLABIES AND NIGHT SONGS by William Engvick

MADELINE by Ludwig Bemelmans

MAKE WAY FOR DUCKLINGS by Robert McCloskey

MOTHER GOOSE: A COLLECTION OF CLASSIC
NURSERY RHYMES by Michael Hague

THE NAPPING HOUSE by Audrey Wood

NOAH'S ARK by Peter Spier

THE OWL AND THE PUSSYCAT by Edward Lear

PETER SPIER'S RAIN by Peter Spier

PLAYING by Helen Oxenbury

THE RANDOM HOUSE BOOK OF MOTHER GOOSE
by Arnold Lobel

READ-ALOUD RHYMES FOR THE VERY YOUNG
by Jack Prelutsky

17 KINGS AND 42 ELEPHANTS by Margaret Mahy

A SNAKE IS TOTALLY TAIL by Judi Barrett

SNUFFY by Dick Bruna

THE TALE OF PETER RABBIT by Beatrix Potter

THE THREE LITTLE PIGS by Paul Galdone

TOMIE DePAOLA'S FAVORITE NURSERY TALES
by Tomie dePaola

THE TOWN MOUSE AND THE COUNTRY MOUSE
by Lorinda Bryan Cauley

THE UGLY DUCKLING by Hans Christian Anderson

THE VERY HUNGRY CATERPILLAR by Eric Carle

WHERE'S SPOT? by Eric Hill

WHO SAID RED? by Mary Serfozo

Great Books for Reading to Preschoolers

ALL GOD'S CRITTERS GOT A PLACE IN THE CHOIR
by Margot Zemach

THE AMAZING VOYAGE OF JACKIE GRACE
by Matt Faulkner

THE AMINAL by Lorna Balian

AMOS AND BORIS by William Steig

BLUEBERRIES FOR SAL by Robert McCloskey

BRINGING THE RAIN TO KAPITI PLAIN:
A NANDI TALE by Verna Aardema

CORDUROY by Don Freeman

CURIOUS GEORGE by H. A. Rey

THE DAY JIMMY'S BOAT ATE THE WASH
by Trinka Hakes Noble

DOCTOR DE SOTO by William Steig

FABLES by Arnold Lobel

FOOLISH RABBIT'S BIG MISTAKE by Rafe Martin

FREDERICK by Leo Lionni

FROG AND TOAD ARE FRIENDS by Arnold Lobel

GEORGE AND MARTHA by James Marshall

GEORGE SHRINKS by William Joyce

THE GREAT BLUENESS AND OTHER
PREDICAMENTS by Arnold Lobel

HARRY AND THE TERRIBLE WHATZIT
by Dick Gackenbach

HECKEDY PEG by Audrey Wood

THE HOUSE ON EAST 88TH STREET
by Bernard Waber

IF I RAN THE ZOO by Dr. Seuss

IRA SLEEPS OVER by Bernard Waber

THE ISLAND OF THE SKOG by Steven Kellogg

JUST SO STORIES by Rudyard Kipling

KATY AND THE BIG SNOW by Virginia Lee Burton

KING BIDGOOD'S IN THE BATHTUB
by Audrey and Don Wood

LITTLE BEAR by Else Holmelund Minarik

THE LITTLE HOUSE by Virginia Lee Burton

LYLE, LYLE CROCODILE by Bernard Waber

MANY MOONS by James Thurber

MIKE MULLIGAN AND HIS STEAM SHOVEL
by Virginia Lee Burton

MILLIONS OF CATS by Wanda Gag

MING LO MOVES THE MOUNTAIN by Arnold Lobel

MISS NELSON IS MISSING by James Marshall

MOUSE TALES by Arnold Lobel

OWL AT HOME by Arnold Lobel

PERFECT THE PIG by Susan Jeschke

PETUNIA by Roger Duvoisin

PRINCESS FURBALL by Charlotte Huck

THE PURPLE COAT by Amy Hest

PUSS IN BOOTS by Charles Perrault

RUMPELSTILTSKIN by Paul O. Zelinsky

THE SEVEN CHINESE BROTHERS by Margaret Mahy

SING A SONG OF PEOPLE by Lois Lenski

THE SNOWY DAY by Ezra Jack Keats

THE STORY ABOUT FERDINAND by Munro Leaf

THE STORY ABOUT PING by Marjorie Flack

SYLVESTER AND THE MAGIC PEBBLE
by William Steig

TELL ME A MITZI by Lore Segal

A THREE HAT DAY by Laura Geringer

THE THREE SILLIES by Kathryn Hewitt

TIKKI TIKKI TEMBO by Arlene Mosel

UNCLE ELEPHANT by Arnold Lobel

WHAT'S THE MATTER WITH CARRUTHERS?
A BEDTIME STORY by James Marshall

WILFRID GORDON MCDONALD PARTRIDGE
by Mem Fox

Great Books for Reading to Kindergartners and First-Graders

ALEXANDER AND THE TERRIBLE, HORRIBLE,
NO GOOD, VERY BAD DAY by Judith Viorst

THE AMAZING BONE by William Steig

AMELIA BEDELIA by Peggy Parish

THE BOY WHO HELD BACK THE SEA
retold by Lenny Hort

BRAVE IRENE by William Steig

A CHAIR FOR MY MOTHER by Vera B. Williams

CHARLOTTE'S WEB by E. B. White

A CHILD'S GARDEN OF VERSES
by Robert Louis Stevenson

CLOUDY WITH A CHANCE OF MEATBALLS
by Judi Barrett

CRANBERRY THANKSGIVING
by Wende and Harry Devlin

DO NOT OPEN by Brinton Turkle

DUFFY AND THE DEVIL by Harve and Margot Zemach

EMILY by Barbara Cooney

EYES OF THE DRAGON by Margaret Leaf

THE 500 HATS OF BARTHOLEMEW CUBBINS
by Dr. Seuss

FLASH, CRASH, RUMBLE AND ROLL
by Franklin M. Branley

GILA MONSTERS MEET YOU AT THE AIRPORT
by Marjorie Weinman Sharmat

THE GIVING TREE by Shel Silverstein

HARALD AND THE GIANT KNIGHT
by Donald Carrick

HENRY BEAR'S PARK by David McPhail

HOW THE MANX CAT LOST ITS TAIL
by Janet Stevens

JANE MARTIN, DOG DETECTIVE by Eve Bunting

KEEP THE LIGHTS BURNING, ABBIE
by Peter and Connie Roop

LITTLE HOUSE IN THE BIG WOODS
by Laura Ingalls Wilder

THE LOST UMBRELLA OF KIM CHU by Eleanor Estes

LOUIS THE FISH by Arthur Yorinks

THE MAGIC SCHOOL BUS series by Joanna Cole

MISS RUMPHIUS by Barbara Cooney

MR. POPPER'S PENGUINS
by Richard and Florence Atwater

THE MOUNTAIN THAT LOVED A BIRD
by Alice McLerran

MUFARO'S BEAUTIFUL DAUGHTERS:
AN AFRICAN TALE by John Steptoe

MY FATHER'S DRAGON by Ruth S. Gannett

NATE THE GREAT by Marjorie Weinman Sharmat

A NEW COAT FOR ANNA by Harriet Ziefert

THE NEW KID ON THE BLOCK by Jack Prelutsky

NOW WE ARE SIX by A. A. Milne

OWL MOON by Jane Yolen

OX-CART MAN by Donald Hall

THE PATCHWORK QUILT by Valerie Flournoy

THE PHILHARMONIC GETS DRESSED by Karla Kuskin

THE POLAR EXPRESS by Chris Van Allsburg

THE PORCELAIN CAT by Michael Patrick Hearn

RAMONA THE PEST by Beverly Cleary

THE RANDOM HOUSE BOOK OF POETRY FOR
CHILDREN by Jack Prelutsky

REGARDS TO THE MAN IN THE MOON
by Ezra Jack Keats

SAM THE MINUTEMAN by Nathaniel Benchley

THE STORY OF THE NUTCRACKER BALLET
by Deborah Hautzig

SING A SONG OF POPCORN: EVERY CHILD'S BOOK
OF POEMS selected by Beatrice Schenk deRegniers,
Eva Moore, Mary M. White, and Jan Carr

STREGA NONA by Tomie dePaola

THE STUPIDS STEP OUT by Harry Allard

SUKEY AND THE MERMAID by Robert D. San Souci

THE SWEETEST FIG by Chris Van Allsburg

TALES OF A GAMBLING GRANDMOTHER by Dayal Kaur Khalsa

THE TALKING EGGS: A FOLKTALE FROM THE AMERICAN SOUTH by Robert D. San Souci

THUNDER CAKE by Patricia Polacco

TOO MANY BOOKS by Caroline Feller Bauer

THE TRUE STORY OF THE 3 LITTLE PIGS by Jon Scieszka

THE VINGANANEE AND THE TREE TOAD by Verna Aardema

WHERE THE SIDEWALK ENDS: POEMS AND DRAWINGS by Shel Silverstein

THE WINTER WREN by Brock Cole

YOU READ TO ME, I'LL READ TO YOU by John Ciardi

Great Books for Reading to Second- and Third-Graders

THE ADVENTURES OF PINOCCHIO by Carlo Collodi

ALL-OF-A-KIND FAMILY by Sidney Taylor

ABEL'S ISLAND by William Steig

THE BAT-POET by Randall Jarrell

THE BEST CHRISTMAS PAGEANT EVER
by Barbara Robinson

THE BFG by Roald Dahl

THE BORROWERS by Mary Norton

THE BRAVE LITTLE TOASTER by Thomas M. Disch

CALL IT COURAGE by Armstrong Sperry

CHARLIE AND THE CHOCOLATE FACTORY
by Roald Dahl

A CHILD'S CHRISTMAS IN WALES by Dylan Thomas

CHOCOLATE FEVER by Robert K. Smith

CLEVER GRETCHEN AND OTHER FORGOTTEN
FOLKTALES by Alison Lurie

THE CHOCOLATE TOUCH by Patrick Skene Catling

A CHRISTMAS CAROL by Charles Dickens

THE COURAGE OF SARAH NOBLE by Alice Dalgliesh

THE CRICKET IN TIMES SQUARE by George Selden

DAWN by Molly Bang

A DOG CALLED KITTY by Bill Walla

HIGGLETY PIGGELTY POP: OR, THERE MUST BE
MORE TO LIFE by Maurice Sendak

THE HUNDRED DRESSES by Eleanor Estes

IN THE YEAR OF THE BOAR AND
JACKIE ROBINSON by Bette Bao Lord

THE IRON GIANT: A STORY IN FIVE NIGHTS
by Ted Hughes

JAMES AND THE GIANT PEACH by Roald Dahl

KNEEKNOCK RISE by Natalie Babbitt

THE MIGHTY SLIDE by Allan Ahlberg

THE MOON'S REVENGE by Joan Aiken

MOSS GOWN by William H. Hooks

THE ORDINARY PRINCESS by M. M. Kaye

OWLS IN THE FAMILY by Farley Mowat

PEARL'S PROMISE by Frank Asch

PETER PAN by J. M. Barrie

THE PIED PIPER OF HAMELIN
retold by Barbara Bartos-Hoppner

PINK AND SAY by Patricia Polacco

PIPPI LONGSTOCKING by Astrid Lingren

RABBIT HILL by Robert Lawson

RAMONA QUIMBY, AGE 8 by Beverly Cleary

THE RELUCTANT DRAGON by Kenneth Grahame

RIP VAN WINKLE
by Washington Irving, retold by John Howe

THE SECRET GARDEN by Frances Hodgson Burnett

THE SHRINKING OF TREEHORN
by Florence Parry Heide

SIDEWAYS STORIES FROM WAYSIDE SCHOOL
by Louis Sachar

THE STORY OF HOLLY AND IVY by Rumer Godden

TINTIN IN TIBET by Herge

THE VELVETEEN RABBIT by Margery Williams

THE WALL by Eve Bunting

WHERE THE BUFFALOES BEGIN by Olaf Baker

WIND IN THE WILLOWS by Kenneth Grahame

WOLF STORY by William McCleery

THE (WONDERFUL) WIZARD OF OZ
by L. Frank Baum

Great Books for Reading to Fourth- and Fifth-Graders

THE ANIMAL FAMILY by Randall Jarrell

THE BEAR'S HOUSE by Marilyn Sachs

BEHIND THE ATTIC WALL by Sylvia Cassedy

BEN AND ME by Robert Lawson

BLUE WILLOW by Doris Gates

BRIDGE TO TERABITHIA by Katherine Paterson

CADDIE WOODLAWN by Carol Ryrie Brink

THE CASE OF THE BAKER STREET IRREGULAR by Robert Newman

CASEY AT THE BAT by Ernest L. Thayer

CHILD OF THE SILENT NIGHT: THE STORY OF LAURA BRIDGMAN by Edith Fisher Hunter

COME SING, JIMMY JO by Katherine Paterson

THE CHRONICLES OF NARNIA by C. S. Lewis

DANNY THE CHAMPION OF THE WORLD by Roald Dahl

DEAR MR. HENSHAW by Beverly Cleary

FIVE CHILDREN AND IT by E. Nesbit

FROM THE MIXED-UP FILES OF MRS. BASIL E. FRANKWEILER by E. L. Konigsburg

GENTLE BEN by Walt Morey

THE GIRL WITH THE SILVER EYES by Willo Davis Roberts

GOOD OLD BOY by Willie Morris

THE GREAT PIRATICAL RUMBUSTIFICATION & THE LIBRARIAN AND THE ROBBERS by Margaret Mahy

HURRY HOME, CANDY by Meindert DeJong

IDA EARLY COMES OVER THE MOUNTAIN by Robert Burch

INTRODUCING SHIRLEY BRAVERMAN by Hilma Wolitzer

KIDNAPPED by Robert Louis Stevenson

LASSIE, COME HOME by Eric Knight

LITTLE WOMEN by Louisa May Alcott

MRS. FRISBY AND THE RATS OF NIMH
by Robert C. O'Brien

MY BROTHER SAM IS DEAD
by James Lincoln Collier and Christopher Collier

MY SIDE OF THE MOUNTAIN by Jean George

NATIONAL VELVET by Enid Bagnold

NORTH TO FREEDOM by Anne Holm

THE RAINBOW PEOPLE by Laurence Yep

SARA CREWE by Frances Hodgson Burnett

THE SEARCH FOR DELICIOUS by Natalie Babbitt

THE SECRET LANGUAGE by Ursula Nordstrom

THE SIGN OF THE BEAVER by Elizabeth George Speare

SING DOWN THE MOON by Scott O'Dell

SKINNYBONES by Barbara Park

SOUNDER by William H. Armstrong

SOUP by Robert Newton Peck

STONE FOX by John R. Gardiner

STORIES FOR CHILDREN by Isaac Bashevis Singer

A TASTE OF BLACKBERRIES by Doris B. Smith

TREASURE ISLAND by Robert Louis Stevenson

TUCK EVERLASTING by Natalie Babbitt

TWENTY AND TEN by Claire H. Bishop

US AND UNCLE FRAUD by Lois Lowry

WHERE THE RED FERN GROWS by Wilson Rawls

THE WHIPPING BOY by Sid Fleischman

THE WITCH OF FOURTH STREET by Myron Levoy

THE WONDERFUL STORY OF
HENRY SUGAR & SIX MORE by Roald Dahl

Great Books for Adults about Great Books for Children

CHILDREN'S BOOKS AND THEIR CREATORS: AN
INVITATION TO THE FEAST OF TWENTIETH-
CENTURY CHILDREN'S LITERATURE
Anita Silvey, Editor. Boston: Houghton Mifflin, 1995.

CHOOSING BOOKS FOR CHILDREN:
A COMMONSENSE GUIDE
By Betsy Hearne. New York: Delacorte Press/Delta, 1990.

FOR READING OUT LOUD! A GUIDE TO SHARING
BOOKS WITH CHILDREN
By Margaret Mary Kimmel and Elizabeth Segel. New York:
Ballantine Books, 1986.

THE NEW YORK TIMES PARENT'S GUIDE TO THE
BEST BOOKS FOR CHILDREN
By Eden Ross Lipson. New York: Times Books/Random
House, 1991.

THE NEW READ-ALOUD HANDBOOK, rev. ed.
By Jim Trelease. New York: Penguin, 1989.

READING FOR THE LOVE OF IT: BEST BOOKS FOR
YOUNG READERS
By Michele Landsberg. New York: Prentice-Hall, 1987.